Cursive Handwriting

8th Grade

Children's Reading & Writing Education Books

Speedy Publishing LLC
40 E. Main St. #1156
Newark, DE 19711
www.speedypublishing.com

Cursive Writing Practice

Practice writing the following sentences and clauses.

(2 Lines)

He was very rich.

The evolution progresses.

My Kinda Girl

I Said I Love You

Never Keeping Secrets

Change The World

Don't break my heart

Take It So Personal

Shower The People

One Tender Moment

Soon as I get home.

The passenger seat.

Love makes things happen

She is all that I need.

It makes me shiver.

She was so excited.

Treat you right.

I'm having lunch.

Wheat bread is better.

Milk is my favorite drink.

He became a soldier.

We look back again.

God called her name.

Respect the life

Respect the life they gave.

God called their name

She never made it home

I hope and pray.

We look back again.

The girl knows her.

Cursive Writing Practice

Practice writing the following sentences and clauses.

(4 Lines)

I heated it in the microwave

She returned the computer

You can always find beauty

He was very rich.

she was bright.

Money cant buy happiness

Keep holding on.

When the cost goes up.

I heated it in the microwave

She returned the computer

You can always find beauty

He was very rich.

she was bright.

Money cant buy happiness

Keep holding on.

When the cost goes up.

Wherever you go?

How are you?

What is your name?

All famous men.

I laid an iron rail.

Sandwich is my favorite.

My dog is my best buddy.

Everyone likes her.

Before you go to bed.

I want some cereal.

Marie likes cats.

Because you were late

A good soccer player.

My soul is grooved.

Her seashell was broken.

We had our first date.

A complete thought.

They cannot stand.

We do not express.

All about the bass.

It gives more information.

Does not keep pace

He hears a different drummer.

She is very complicated.

I heard from your mom.

Your daddy loves you

I know you feel scared

The evolution progresses.

Cursive Writing Practice

Write the paragraph taken from the famous novel **“A Tale of Two Cities” by Charles Dickens (1859)**

A Tale of Two Cities

by Charles Dickens 1859

It was the best of times,

it was the worst of times,

it was the age of wisdom,

it was the age of foolishness,

it was the epoch of belief,

it was the epoch of incredulity

it was the season of Light,

it was the spring of hope,

it was the winter of despair,

we had everything before us,

we had nothing before us,

we were all going to heaven,

we were all going direct

the other way – in short,

the period was so far like the

present period,

that some of its noisiest

authorities insisted on its being

received, for good or for evil,

in the superlative degree of

comparison only.

www.ingramcontent.com/pod-product-compliance
Lightning Source LLC
LaVergne TN
LVHW082306150826
845677LV00009B/1735

* 9 7 9 8 8 6 9 4 4 8 9 2 7 *